Who Am I?

Where Did I Come From?

Where Am I Going?

by

Dr. David E. Fritsche Sr Th. D.

Who Am I?

Where Did I Come From?

Where Am I Going?

By

Dr. David E. Fritsche Sr. Th. D.

A special thanks to Donna Krecklow, who edited this manuscript. Without her expertise and encouragement this work would simply be a mess. Thank You Donna!

Dynamix Worx Publications

ISBN-13: 9798716284012

Dedication:

To my family

To Mom & Dad, who loved us enough to expect the highest and best. Who put up with our antics and struggles, kept a secure and unchangeable fence of expectations around us and never gave up.

To Laila, Sharon and Donna, my sisters in crime who made life an adventure and made me better than I might have been.

To Linda, my sister's friend who hung out at our house and then became my wife, best friend and the mother of our three children.

To my children, David Jr., Robert and Alycia who were and are a delight and who now rule the world as children of light, beacons of success and examples of life well lived.

Who Am I? Where Did I Come From? Where Am I Going?

Prologue

I was raised in church by a God honoring family. From my
earliest memories come visions of being in church,
singing, listening to sermons, even before I had any
conscious knowledge of what was said. I do not resent
that context for my life. Not at all. Sure, there are things
to unlearn, and things that today make no sense at all.
But by and large it was a healthier setting than some I
watched in my peers and has given me some moral
structure to wrestle with and to either affirm or leave
behind. It was a good point of beginning.

There was much emphasis in the churches we attended
on finding and knowing the will of God for our lives. Of
course, if you do not believe in the existence of God, then
that probably seems trite and meaningless. But it was
emphasized. I can remember many sermons on finding
the will of God and following it, and not a few that
dangled us precariously over the pit, warning that if you
come to a fork in the road of life and choose the wrong
direction, you would forever be remanded to failure, or at
best, second place in your true potential. The concept of
missing God's best was terrifying and sparked sheer terror
to the hearers. It was not until my late teens that I began
to question the basis of this terror and came to a
revolutionary conclusion. The Bible and God is not about
our doing the will of God but about our BEING the will of
God. It was a revelation born out of a new concept: God
does not exist in a time and space continuum, but is
timeless and without beginning and end. All things are
thus present tense to God. He is alpha and omega, the

beginning and the end. If that is true, then the events of our lives are just an accumulation of expressions of what we are. The issues of God are eternal; therefore, He is not concerned with the events of our lives as much as with our coming into personal maturity in 'being.' It is what we are that is the focus of the will of God. The events are simply expressions of our being, our character and our sense of self.

In the following pages we will explore the meaning of life and of the quest for personal identity. I promise, I will not dangle you over the pit of hell and give you the impossible task of knowing now what you cannot know until you've been there. That is much of what life is about. It is about your development and your responses to the creative genius that is YOU!

So, relax and take a trip with me. We will challenge some assumptions of our modern culture and hopefully you will find freedom to be what God has created you to be. In that quest, you will hear a phrase several time. It is the key phrase of existence: You cannot become what you already are. Way too much energy has gone into the pressure of finding yourself, as pop-psychology says it, and far too little into the enjoyment of life and the journey of realizing what you already are in God's view.

Ready? OK, here we go...

Chapter 1

Who do you think you are?

I grew up before television, computers and a host of modern time occupying technological conveniences. Washing machines had wringers on the side. They did not go through cycles, they just sat there and swished. The real work was done by the housewife who attended them. The ice man came every other day and you put a card in the window to indicate if you needed some for your icebox. The milk man came daily also, but he passed by our house because we had a cow. Come to think about it, he passed by many of our neighbors also, for old Bessie made enough milk for us and much of the neighborhood.

We played games as kids. Some were well known but many we just made up as we went along. For we boys, there were the radio program heroes to emulate in our play. Yes, all the boys had guns and played cowboys and Indians. Sammy, down the street was always Tonto and I was always The Lone Ranger.

As you can see, I grew up with certain stereotypical assumptions about life. Boys and girls were different and our roles in life were assumed to be different. Sorry for the gender identity assumptions Mr. Modern psychologist, but you'll also have to forgive me for observing that the criminal statistics and lack

of personal identity issues of our day might just show that our assumptions protected us from a lot of conflict and trouble.

So, we played and assimilated certain values from the heroes of the day, like truthfulness, honor, moral high ground and so forth. It was all there in the pictures the radio painted for the images in our imagination.

Of course, all that has changed. Today's most popular icons of our young people are tainted, conflicted, in-your-face freaks, who live on the edge of sanity and invite their followers to join in the daring quest to destroy the morality of the past, reframe the ethics of goodness and discover by experimentation the joys of rehabilitation and insanity.

And we wonder why it is that today's youth are confused, wayward, and without a sense of who they are and where they are going...

Let's stop here on our journey and look back, not just to the world I grew up in but before that. Our world has changed as has our view of reality. Just 100 or so years ago, 97% of our population was busy in the enterprise of agriculture. OK, let's look at the world before that...

Although human social structures have not always been stereotypical, sociologists propose a picture of human progress as starting with the Hunter-Gatherer. These neo-caveman figures spent all of their time foraging for food, gathering what they could and then moving on to new ground to do the same. 100% of their time was given to the tasks of survival and the gathering of food.

Somewhere along the way, some wise guy observed that some places brought forth more food than others. This wise guy, or wise girl, as the case may be, observed that plants grew from seeds and the more seeds that were planted the more plants grew. They also observed that more plants attracted more animals, and life was good for the Hunter-Gatherer when such a place was found.

This shift of world view was monumental. When it was accepted, everything changed. Instead of moving from place to place to find food, the tribe found the best land they could and started planting and growing rather than traveling and gathering. The age of agriculture was born. It also meant that the roles people played in life changed. The men began the regular work of cultivating rather than hunting as a singular focus. Boys spent their time with Dad in the fields and of necessity, Mom and the girls were at home preparing and preserving that which was being grown. It was better and easier than was life on the move.

The family also changed. From being a tribe of related generations, the social group became the nuclear family,  with mother, father, and the children born to their union. Their relationships were close, of necessity, for they were together all the time. The boys were in the field with dad and the girls were around the house and barn with mom.

Let's stop here and take a look at this social structure
more closely. Joe, short for Joseph, is the oldest of the six
boys. And Jane is the oldest of the six girls. OK, there were
probably more girls than boys as is the nature of birth
statistics, but for the sake of our story, we will simply
divide them evenly. Twelve children? Why yes, of course.
You see, 100 years ago of more, there were no
contraceptives and no televisions or computers, so mom
and dad were together every evening with nothing more
to do than make babies. Besides, with the work of the
farm, and more helping hands available, the more work
could be done and the more crops and animals could be
produced.

So, families were large and of the 20 people in this family
– Ah, yes, 20! Let's count them. Mom and dad make 2, +
the twelve children make 14, plus grandma & grandpa
make 16. They have to have somewhere to live, for they
are already in their mid-50's and they may not last much
longer. Grandpa fell a couple of years back and broke his
hip and it didn't heal right and there is no such thing as a
hip replacement. And Grandma? Well, she forgets things
a lot and there is not social services or government
programs to put her in a home somewhere, so she stays
also.

But that's only 16! How did we get to 20? Well don't forget Aunt Edith and her two children. They had to go somewhere when Uncle Elmer died in the Indian raid years ago. The Indians, you see, did not take to the agricultural lifestyle easily, for their traditions and heritage was firmly rooted in the hunter-gatherer world. So, when they came to take the calf from the farm for food, they thought they were finding available food and Uncle Elmer thought they were thieves. So, he went out to stop them and they, being hungry and all, just killed him and rode away.

So, we have 16 people in the house with grandma and grandpa, plus Aunt Edith and her two children, and, oh yes, we almost forgot, there is Uncle Elmer's mother who was living with them and she has to have a place to live also. So, there we are – 20 people.

But how do you feed 20 people in one house? Not really a problem. Everyone has their tasks, depending on their age and ability and it is still pretty much a matter of survival. You work, you raise, you harvest, you can the fruits and vegetables for the winter food, and you have no leisure time for TV, computers, organized sports or other things. It is just as well, for the modern means of entertainment that we enjoy today did not exist anyway. Al Gore had not invented the internet yet nor man made global warming. The issues of life were simple; work and eat and sleep and get up at dawn and do it again.

Identity? Who am I? I might suggest here that the question never came to mind. That issue came with TV and computers. Before our modern age of technology and the industrial revolution, the answer was assumed from birth so it never became an issue in the teen years. 93% of the population were engaged in the task of agriculture and almost 100% of that was the family farm. So, the question of identity was a given. The boys were going to grow up, find a pretty young girl within the 20 to 30 girls that they met in their teen years and get married. The choices for a wife, by today's standards will be limited to a half dozen girls in the community school house that are anywhere near Joe's age, plus a few in the community church and the few that might come from the other community over the mountain to the county fair.

Joe and his new wife will stake out some plot of ground in the valley that looked good for farming or take a section (640 acres) from mom and dad's farm and it would all start over again. Joe will be a farmer, have a wife and a dozen children and ultimately take care of mom and dad and any other strays that came along with the family history.

But why doesn't Aunt Edith and grandpa and grandma go one welfare or social security or Obama Care? For the same reason that the family does not watch much TV or socialize with their friends on their iPhone – There isn't any!

So, the available choices of identity are very limited. One, or possibly two of the 12 children will escape the farm and move to the city where the other 7% of the population reside and will try their hand at being a merchant, a blacksmith, a sheriff or some other related, equally difficult task. Life is simple, work is hard and **<u>identity is provided – it is not chosen.</u>**

Let me say that again. **<u>Identity is provided – it is not chosen.</u>** What you are and will be is not questioned. You work or you don't eat. If you do not carry your load, no one will carry it for you. Is this a hard harsh conservative Republican setting? No, politics has little to do with it. It is a matter of social structures and survival. Everyone works of necessity and **<u>identity is in the work.</u>** Personal responsibility is not a choice, it is an essential element of survival. You either take responsibility for your place on the farm or 19 other people will be watching, waiting and will see to it that you function.

Chapter 2

Times change and so do the questions

But we do not live back then, you say. Agreed! Just thought it might be important to catch a perspective of how we got to this point in civilization and how it has altered our questions about life and identity.

Somewhere in the shifting world views of the past, some other wise guy decided that what their farm produced was not the same as what another farm produced across the valley and specialization was born. With it came greater reliance on trading specialized labor, focus and production, leading to the industrial age and the move of the family from the farm into the city. Again, with the shift of world view and the scope of alternative lifestyles it offered, everything changed. Just in the past 100-150 years of human history, we have seen more social structure changes than in the entire rest of preceding human history. From the life of the nomadic hunter-gatherer, to the world of agriculture and the family farm, we have shifted from 93% of the population living on the family farm to 97% living in the city. And the few who remain in the task of agriculture produce far more for us to eat than the previous world where 93% worked at it. So, the questions of who am I and of identity change also.

The industrial revolution opened great possibilities to the nation, but it also changed the picture of the family. Dad was no longer in the field with the boys, he was in the factory alone, with other dads who left the home for long periods of time to work with other dads away from home. And mom was no longer working 22 hours a day cooking, cleaning and canning. Factories and stores took care of the production of things to eat and so mom's life changed forever also.

Joe, in our new industrial world, went off to school as did Jane and they now had fewer siblings to compete with for food at the table. Grandma

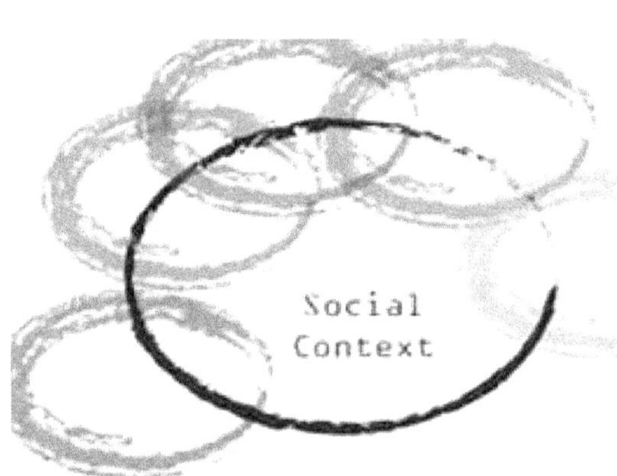

and grandpa lived longer and may be living alone, but nearby. School now took up a greater portion of Joe's and Jane's life and they met far more children from which to choose a husband or wife. Their perspective of their future also changed. Joe did not have to settle on the necessary agricultural life. He could become a factory worker, a mechanic, a delivery driver or any other number of things. He had more choices, but by today's standards, they were still limited.

So off to school Joe and Jane went, and they were met by the teachers and asked, "What do you want to be when you grow up?" The question was never a part of life in the agricultural age. And Joe, and/or Jane would inevitably answer, "I don't know!" I mean with so many choices, who would know at a young age. And the question loomed large in grade school, junior high school and high school. It would continue in college, but only a small percentage of the industrial age children would go to college. Their necessary skills for that age would be shaped by an apprenticeship, on the job training or possibly with the dull boring routine of the assembly line, putting widgets on thingamabobs.

The world wars also shaped the profile of the family and the roles each played. The need for production and the raising of an army of men, left many industrial tasks to the women of the world. So eventually, both mom and dad were out of the home for long periods of the day and Joe and Jane were left to the influences of the school and their peers. The family was changing and so were the roles, identities and lives as the work and activities of the day determined the individual's identity.

But there were more choices. Joe and Jane were periodically tested to see what their occupational skills were. School became increasingly specialized also, so that the one room school house was reduced to a footnote in ancient history. Classes were specialized and taught by specialized teachers. Joe and Jane grew up, in this time, in the pursuit of a specialized education for a specialized life. The only problem was, when they graduated from high school, no one cared about their specialty. The school had said, "We like to think of each of our students as an individual, each like a flower, blooming in their own way and in their own time." But upon graduation, the factory hired them and did not say, "We like to think of all of our employees as a little flower, each blooming in its own way and in its own time." The factory said something more like, "Here's your time card. Punch in at 7 A.M. do your routine task and punch out at 4 P.M. Bring your lunch, because we do not feed you, test you or take care of you. You are no longer an individual, you are part of the industrial machinery!"

But again, that was the past and this is now. Life may not be better but it is different. The questions of identity and value and self-worth can now be asked, but I wonder if the answers are any better than in ages past? The larger question may be, are we better people because of our greater available choices? In the past we did not ask where we were going to live, what we would do for our life's work or what was our identity. Our identity was more a matter of observing what others thought of us, how they identified us and what we did to produce a living. There was no question of occupational identity, group identity, sexual identity, or many of the things that now have associations, power bases, sub-cultural icons and other means of 37 levels of sub-identities. In the past, we simply did not ask the questions for the answers were assumed without question.

Today's Joe and Jane have to find a sub-structural style of music that is a sub-style of an alternative style of a distinct but similar genre of a subset of noises. They also have to choose a style of dress that is distinct to the musical choices and the sub-group within the group, that is distinct to the expectations of the peer group, which makes them unique from the rest of the world, making a statement that they are different, but all the same also. They have to decide if they are hetero-sexual, homo-sexual, bi-sexual, trans-sexual, tri-sexual or other terms I have never heard of before. They also have to guard that identity carefully, relating to others in the peer group with absolute and total acceptance or their difference, but united in their total rejection of anyone who is not tolerant. The mantra is, "If there anything I cannot stand it is intolerant people!"

If all that sounds confusing, it is only because it is. We have left the security of the past in which many questions of identity were never asked, to a day in which all the questions are asked but no assumptions provide guidelines to our lives. The end result is not a better person or a better society. The end result is the breakdown of the structures of the past that provided security, direction and identity by where and how we functioned. The end result is a cacophony of sounds, sights, alternatives and confusion, with no definition and no future.

The question is: What will the social structures of the future be? Will there be a family, a definable occupation, a peer group or a philosophical norm? Is our society making progress or are we coming to the place that we have lost all sense of any structure, tradition, expectation of normalcy? Is being abnormal the new "in" thing of identity and if so, then are we headed to a culture clash, when there are no new 'abnormal' left with which to

identify? I mean, if you have to be different and have to
be accepted because of your difference, then where do
we go from absolute chaotic identity confusion?

Chapter 3

Finding some basic structure

The basic structure of humanity, from the beginning of time, has been the nuclear family. Today it is under assault. Its traditional structure of a man (husband) and woman (wife), is being challenged. Certainly we, with our modern genius, can do better than God in starting this whole thing with Adam and Eve and the entire rest of human history. We are modern, smart, educated, diverse, accepting, and elite on knowing far more than the rest of humanity that preceded us and, of course, than God Himself. (Sarcasm intended)!

So, we can redefine the basic elements of the foundational structure of the human relationship and…

We do not have to have a man and woman married in traditional roles and sacred oaths. A family can be anything you want it to be – Right? Marriage can also be anything you want it to be with whomever or whatever you want it to be – Right?

But at the risk of being seen as a bigoted old Neanderthal, who certainly should be rejected by those who are intolerantly intolerant, to what end do we need to redefine and restructure human relationships? If we abandon the possibilities of reproduction in our relationships, are we nor relegating humanity to extinction? If we answer "no, there will always be those who reproduce" then we are accepting the norm as the un-norm, and making place for the intolerant in a world of pseudo-tolerance, which is, by its very nature – intolerant. Does all this sound confusing? It only sound confusing because it is.

We have confused progress with the need to abandon tried and true principles of human relationship. We have borrowed the words and institutions developed by the church over thousands of years and decided that we want to own those words and recreate their definitions. "Family," "Marriage," and a host of other traditional terms and meanings are under fire, not because we have a more perfect definition but because we want our abnormal to be accepted, not as a moral equivalent but as morally superior. We do not want our individual role in life to be seen as, well, an individual and personal identity. We want to find some advantage in it, some glory in it and some notice that make it better to be different than it is to be traditionally normal. Again, does this sound confusing? Of course, it does, only because it is.

If those who want to relate to themselves and their few sub-cultural peers in some alternative way want an identity for it, call it whatever you want but for goodness sakes, do not try to steal perfectly good definitions for relationships that have existed since the beginning of time. The official state government borrowed the terms "Marriage" and "Family" from the traditions of the church. They need to give them back and stop redefining.

It is too confusing. So have a ceremony for you and your dog and call the union a Barrage, or a Canine Communal Suffrage, or whatever you want, but is it really good for the human social structures to destroy the concepts and formation of the past? Is it OK to conclude that there is and was a normal traditional world in which structures existed that worked and that if we do not want to live within those traditional structures, we bear the responsibility for the resulting upheaval in our world, not those who intolerantly follow the tried-and-true structures that have sustained civilization since the beginning of time?

The traditional family structure has much to recommend it. No, it does not accommodate a lot of things that are acceptable in our modern world. It should not. It is, at its very core a structure of normalcy that contains expectations of identity and roles and values that work to provide a context for life. Without that context, chaos is the result.

Everyone needs some structure and expectation in life. Those structures are the fabric of personal worth, individual dreams and goals and the support structure for our future. I remember driving to Eugene, Oregon one day. My sisters had called. My dad had gotten up early as was his custom, and fallen. Mom came to see what had happened only to find him dead beside his bed. A sudden heart attack had ended his life.

The call came as I was going to a men's retreat and I was the main speaker. I started to turn around and return home to call and cancel my journey and start moving toward Eugene instead. Then a correction came to my mind. No, that is not what dad would want. He would want me to handle my responsibility, do my duty and then come to take care of his affairs. So, I went to the conference, told them of my emotional plight and spoke. It was one of the high points of my ministry. Old hurts, family disagreements and personal damage in the men at the conference were exposed and dealt with as never before.

I finished the couple of days of teaching and then headed for Eugene. On the way I had a lot to think about. Dad was not just a good guy; he was my hero and a giant among men. His pastoral ministry in our church was an example to me of the highest of ethic, honor and truth. I was grateful for my parents and for the family they provided. I was honored by the structures they provided and for the residual effects of those structures in my life.

I thought much about the expectation dad had for me. They were high expectations. He never allowed me to stray from doing things right and from a sense of excellence in all that I did. He never pushed me to be what he was or to choose the occupation he chose, but there were moral and ethical parameters to my life that were placed there by a loving but insistent father who wanted the best for his children.

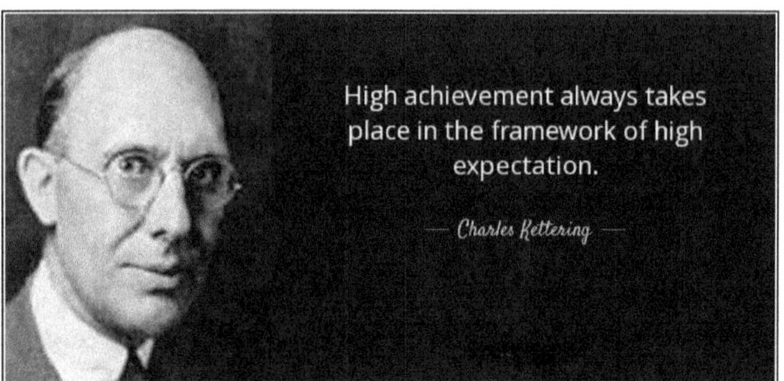

Then I started laughing. The thought that struck me funny was that dad was gone now and I did not have to live up to his expectations or his exacting standards. I could now live and I pleased and he could not be disappointed because he was gone. Then the laughter subsided as I began to weep again. I would not change my life, abandon my principles nor change my lifestyle. I had been shaped by those expectations, defined by those values and trained to those perceptions. They were no longer the context of my family – <u>they were me!</u>

Parents do their children no favor by being overly permissive, accepting of weirdness and tolerant of less than the exceptional. Just as the work of the past generations created the identity and definition of life, so also does the structure of the family provide for the ethical, moral and standards of excellence in the child. Those who are too weak to train, instruct and confront as parents are inviting an end result of lack of identity, context and security that will destroy the child when it is the adult.

It may be possible that what we see as cultural confusion in our day, is less the fault of the wayward and aimless child and more the fault of a weak and permissive parent who was too insecure in themselves to believe that they had anything to offer of right and wrong, acceptable and unacceptable or of what the parent is there for – to create an identity and foundation for the child, rather than leave the child to figure it out without any structures to rely on. This is not love! Not love at all!

Years ago, I was privileged to attend a practice of the Santa Clara Swim Team. The coach was running up and down the side of the pool, shouting and challenging. "You can go one second faster. GO, GO, GO! Come on, you can do this!" One would have thought the team would hate him. But a few days later, as they were competing in the world finals, the team was gathered around him with tears running down their faces as they held the metals for new world records.

I do not know how many kids left the team because of the high pressure and high standards, but for those who did not, there were gold metals to be had, records to be set and a sense of pride in their accomplishments. Some people and parents think that their children will love them if they are easy on them, expect nothing and allow them to do as they please. Quite the contrary. Our kids gain strength from us and love for us when we set high expectations and then do not allow them to fail.

What we are not advocating is brutality, anger, rage, negativity and abuse in some twisted application of parenting or coaching. To demean or intimidate is not the same as challenging and raising the expectations and confidence of our youth. The point is that our involvement as parents and leaders must not pander to the lowest they are capable of but to their highest and best.

The world is a difficult place, filled with temptations to failure, pressures to quit and peer pressure to go down paths that lead only to hell. Competition for the highest and the best is fierce and only those who face life with confidence and strength will survive. We live in a world that has become permissive, value free, accepting of low levels of effort and non-judgmental of all things. We have become a nation of wimps; whose main accomplishment is to get a government check or subsidy. We have demonized competition, accomplishment and the success of those who have more than others. We have elected leaders who are without vision, without strength and who want to take care of everyone rather than challenge them to excel. We have lowered the bar of what we expect and reduced the expectation of our next generation. Why? For goodness sakes, WHY?

Chapter 4

Challenging Principles

If we believe that mankind is created in the image of God and by God, then there are certain assumptions that we hold. We hold that, inherent in the creative scheme is the wherewithal to do what the Creator designed. There is also an assumption that if the Creator tells us to do something or not do something, then it is a good thing to do or not do.

Whether or not you believe in God, you will acknowledge that there are laws in this universe which govern the actions of nature. The laws of nature are universally held and as we understand them, we affirm that they work in a certain framework and with predictable accuracy. To violate the laws of nature is to bring pain into our lives. If you jump off of a tall building, you can change your mind half way down and repent, but the law of natural consequences it at play and you will hit the ground. The law of gravity will see to it.

Principles are simply those things that we understand that act like and through the laws of nature. They are truths that have been learned by experience and have been codified for our benefit. It is the principles of the Founding Fathers of this nation that have laid the groundwork for our exceptionalism. This nation is not great because we are better than any other people or because God just arbitrarily pointed His finger at the planet and decided to give us more of everything. We are great, not because God is on our side, but because we have, lived by the principles laid down in our foundations, been on God's side. Blessings are released by right principles.

A Look at the Law

The law is simply the codification of principles, set to accompanying penalties to safeguard our world. Well, that is what they should be at least. The law prescribes penalties to warn us and frighten us from breaking the law. But good laws, designed to protect us, cannot, in reality be broken. That is, you cannot really break the law of gravity. It survives quite well even when we ignore it. What is broken is the violator. The law breaks the violator. There are consequences to the ignoring of the law, or ethical standards, principles and traditional norms that have been given for our protection.

Traditions are the fabric of past generations and their experience in the order of the universe. They can seem silly, errant and mischievous, but they are there because of past realizations of truth. Not all folklore or old wife's tales are

truth. But there are traditional values and ethical standards that, like the law, warn us of danger and are there to protect us.

We live in a modern world that seems hell bent on challenging everything of the past and of redesigning our ethical and moral world. While challenging assumptions has value in science and in education, there are principles and traditions that need to be affirmed rather than cast away without regard. Yes, the world is changing and looking at everything that was considered reality is the seed plot of progress, it is not wise to simply disregard the entire body of ethical and moral values passed down by those who have gone before.

We appear to be moving governmentally away from the free market into another experiment with socialism and the communal philosophies that have failed so miserably in the past. Our blindness to the lessons of history does not mean that we will finally find a way to make past failed social systems work. It will ultimately mean that we will experience the failures of the past and learn from experience that which we would not learn by tradition and history. Yes, we will learn old lessons again, but at the cost of personal and social damage that need not be.

So also, with the ethical and moral underpinnings of the past. You can castigate past generations for being too up-tight, too rigid, and too religious, too anything, but their traditional forms, beliefs and systems have brought us great success and protected us from great harm to this point. To the degree that we insist on throwing away traditional social systems, ethical expectations and moral guidelines, we can be certain of damage because of our violations to some degree – great or small.

One of the calls of today is to do away with victimless crimes. You know, if it is private behavior and everyone is consenting and no one else knows, "what is the harm," they say! No harm – no foul! But there is no objective measurement for the emotional damage done to relationships, to families, to friendships, to reputations, to others who may not know, but who will know at an emotional level and probably find out sometime anyway. That which is right and ethical and moral needs no secrecy. Only sin requires the cover of darkness.

While our modern world paints the sophisticated picture of the non-conformist, there is something to be said for conforming to those principles and traditions that are there to save our hide.

Chapter 5

The Search for Moral Equivalency

It is that body of definition (our ethical position, our moral stance, our traditional acceptance and the law) that defines us and determines our destiny. How we will act, what we will do and not do, what we aspire to and how we relate to our world is the primary source of our sense of self.

A nation exists when there is culture, language and boarders. The culture is its values, its ethical stance, its heart, if you will. A culture exists when there are traditional issues to which it ascribes and that govern its thinking. The language is that common interaction by which it communicates its social life. Its boarders are those parameters that exist to define its territory, its land, and its holdings. So also, an individual exists when there is definition of those three things: our traditions and the social relationships we choose to be with and to be like, our language in communicating with that group and our chosen personal boarders.

Yes, those things do not exist in a vacuum nor are they imposed by some twist of fate. They are chosen. We choose our identity and we choose how we will live in our world. That is the issue of personal responsibility – what I am is determined! If that basic premise is missing from our assumptions of self, then we are not responsible. We are increasingly seeing the dismissal of personal responsibility in our culture by the rejection of that premise. "I am not responsible, it's just the way I am," has become a legal defense from violations of the law, from personal responsibility and

from ethical constraints. The counter (opposing) sub-cultures of our world increasingly feel the need to flaunt their difference (irresponsibility) in the face of the law, our ethics, and our traditional values and in a fit of passion, demand acceptance, not for any contribution to the culture or nation but because of their difference. That is, "I'm weird and I demand to be accepted, not for my being a part of the world in which I live or any contribution to it, but because I am weird." This we call the demand for moral equivalency.

Parameters are the essence of a nation, a culture or any definable group. Corporation have a constitution and by-laws to set in legal terms, what they are and what they do. Religions define themselves by their ethical and moral tone and the traditions in which they believe. Clubs define their purpose and the activities that they will engage in. Every sport has rules and penalties that set the stage for the competition. So also, with an individual. Each individual set for themselves the definitions of culture, language and boarders that will give them access into their world.

Our world has become a confusing mixture of sub-culture and sub-sub-cultures, each competing for some definition that is aside from the national culture, and each demanding equality. These all misinterpret our national constitution and its statement of "all men are created equal…" to mean that the culture has to accept not only me as a biological entity but all the choices I make in contradistinction to the main culture. We seem to feel that we can reject everything in the culture and still demand parity. But the very existence of parameters means that some things are acceptable and some things are not. Equality before the law does not mean that I can demand equality of behavior or economics or anything else, in contrast to the law. Again, you do not break the law, the law breaks you!

We are caught in a moral dilemma in which the rejection of the differences has become the primary sin of our accepting and patronizing world. Nothing should be judged, rejected or criticized, for we have a right to be weird. But that is the very essence and role of definition. It excludes. It rejects that which it sees as a threat to the definition that creates its existence. A religion cannot exist without its beliefs and ethical and moral context. To do so is to destroy the fabric of the religion. The same goes for any definable entity, any group and any nation. It is not just that we have definition but that the definition determines something. It exists to be the context for the life we live and the goals we have and the direction we are headed. The fall out is, it demands conformity and adherence to its parameters.

It is in this lack that our nation has lost its way. We have lost any definition in the push for multiculturalism. What we were, is the melting pot for people, leaving their nation and culture to become Americans. What we end up with is a stew, in which the transportation of other cultures, value systems and ethical consideration demand acceptance rather than becoming renewed into a new culture. This is also true for the sub-cultures that vie for acceptance. We have become a place in which our sexual orientation, our race, our gender, our appearance, our condition, our economics, our disease, our... - difference, is the identity, not our context within the greater whole. We are not melting – we are competing. We are competing for notice, rewards, revenues and status not based on our contribution to the defined culture but because of our contrast to the culture. The nation and the culture cannot exist as long as we are focused on the demands for moral equivalency based on our being outside of the parameters, or having no parameters.

The end result is that the definition of normalcy and the culture ceases to exist and chaos ensues. The end result is not that the difference is accepted as equivalent, but without some difference in contradistinction to the norm and the definition of the whole, you have no definition. In the accepting of anything and everything, that which comprised the definition is lost. What then exists is not moral equivalent, but morally superior. The weird rule and the definition are lost because the greatest sin of all and the only thing rejected is rejection and definition itself.

OK, yes! Definition, rules and ethical stances require rejection, judgment and that is what holds the structure together. For the individual, that is what creates a sense of self and of worth and of a future. Without that definition we are adrift in a sea of confusion and blown by the winds of the next weird trend. Interesting that the

more people group together in their latest pop weirdness
to be different, the more they seem the same. Is it of
value to reject the tried-and-true foundations of
traditional definitions simply to be accepted outside the
camp? What is it in us that makes us want to reject
normalcy as defined in our culture for something else? Is
the search for identity so difficult that we have to find
some difference to define us, rather than to set about to
contribute to our world?

But didn't Jesus say we are not to judge one another? Yes,
of course. Well, what He really said was that we were not
to judge, lest we are also judged. What He did not imply
was that we should invite the destruction of the definition
of our religion, club or culture on the altar of 'difference.'
The context is in our treatment of the sinner not in our
acceptance of the sin. Normalizing sin (behavior outside
of the parameter) destroys the context, which destroys
the culture.

How many families have been torn apart by the behavior
of one, who demands to go their own way, do their own
thing and the effect on the rest be damned? How many
organizations have ceased to exist because they could not
define their purpose and determine their direction? Yes,
definition is an essential ingredient in creating a culture
and it is an essential ingredient in creating and
maintaining a person also.

Chapter 6

The Search for Self

Many years ago now, a lady came to me for counseling. She had problems. She was married to her fifth husband and had been involved in as many as 10 affairs outside of each of those five marriages. Her question for me and her objective in counseling was to help her learn how to select the right man. In 50 men, she had chosen bad guys. That left me with quite a task.

I started by suggesting that possibly, in 50 men there was one average Joe who would make at least a low-level acceptable husband. But it was a tough sell. She insisted that they were all inadequate as husbands and possibly as human beings. So, we started by asking her to make a list of the things she did not like about her current husband. She started writing... The end result was 10 pages, single spaced, both sides of the paper. I put the list in her file and we continued with other things.

At the end of a year of counseling I asked her to repeat the exercise. She did. One page, five items. Then I asked her what percentage of the whole of her husband was comprised by those five items. She answered that it was about 10%. I then asked if she were to refocus her attention to the 90% of value and worth that he represented, if the marriage might be better. She laughed and that concluded the counseling.

But let's back up about six months. There was an incident that was a turning point in the process. One day she arrived at the office without an appointment asking for just a minute of my time. She wanted to say good-by, for she was leaving. She was tired of the constraints, of the imposed expectations from her children, her parents, her husband and her friends. She was going to throw it all off and go away by herself to find herself.

Knowing the language of the pop psychology of the day, I asked her what other counselor she had been seeing. She acknowledged that she had been seeing another counselor. I was not offended, but thought it consistent with her fidelity to her husbands through the years. I laughed as she asked, "How did you know?"

Then I asked where she was going? She was ambivalent, not knowing for sure. She had just thrown her clothes and some personal belongings in her car and was on her way. I asked if she was going to Barstow? Barstow is a hot barren community in the Mojave Desert. "No! Why would I go there?" she replied. Then I asked if she was going to Siberia? Again, she answered no, emphatically. Question marks filled her face as I asked about other out of the way places. Then I said, "I assume, since you are driving, that you are not going to Hawaii but possibly to Southern California." She acknowledged that she was thinking that might be the best place to go, walk on the beach and sort things out and find herself.

Then I asked, how she would know when she found herself? Again, she looked at me quizzically. So, I asked, "I mean, will you be walking along the beach and stumble over something, stop, pick it up, brush the sand off of it and there, behold will be yourself?" She indicated that she had not thought about the details, just that she had to go away and find herself. Then a look of confusion filled her face.

I continued. "What if you discover that you are really an onion?" She laughed, but the question marks on her face intensified. "What if, after pealing back all the  layers of implied expectations of your husband, children, church, parents, etc., you discover that there is nothing left? What if your relationship to yourself without context is non-existent?" I asked.

At this point, she began to cry. She was trapped and she knew it and she had no answers. Then I started to rebuild the concept of the problem. The problem was not that others had destroyed her but that she had failed to determine for herself what her own definition was. She had assumed, as does the majority of our modern world, that self is something out there, something that you experience outside of you, something that is found in experimentation, in some transcendent revelation or mystical revelation.

Then I suggested that self cannot be found it has to be created. God does not throw us onto the planet with a self-portrait hidden somewhere for us to find. He makes us as a blank canvas, then gives us paints and brushes and asks us to paint ourselves. Selfhood is a matter of our making. It is determined, not found. Yes, we have a certain set of genetic skills, talents and desired. Those are the paint and the brushes. It is our responsibility to create the finished picture. This is the essence of personal responsibility. This is the fabric of context, definition and the individual culture that we fit into. This is the process of life: Creating me and determining what I will contribute to my world. This is the self-sufficiency that is so clearly lacking in our day, as we look to our difference to define us rather than to our internal character to guide us. This is the answer to our search for self in a contrasting sub-culture or a contrasting difference or in something outside of our self. Our self is not out there. It is in here. It is not defined by our weirdness but by our contribution. It is not found, it is created. It is not the government's job to define us, to take care of us, or to create a new arena of acceptance based on our difference. It is the governments job to defend our rights to create ourselves, not to reward us for our not having the responsibility to create something worthwhile.

The message is simple and the task is clear. Stop waiting for the context, club, church, world, or government to accept you and promote a sense of self for you. Get busy creating yourself. Set some goals, dream some dreams, make some plans, venture into the unknown world of possibilities and develop your skills. While you are waiting for yourself to come knocking on your door and announce that it is here, go to school and get involved in a context, a club, a church and discover that the self you wait for is within you to create.

Unless we can turn this philosophical corner and start moving into a national identity and culture, this social experiment we call America is over. As long as we dance around to the cause of multiculturalism, compete for acclaim and acceptance based on our difference and allow for time, money and our national energy to be expended in this search for self, we are doomed to the total erosion of our parameters, our culture and our national foundations. A family cannot exist without a central sense of identity. A nation cannot either. A person who is adrift on the sea of self and who expects the world to bend to its difference, is delusional and if the world attempts to solve the problem, the world will go down with that individual.

Wake up folks! You are who you are because you created you. If you are unhappy, start pursuing happiness by defining your own direction and your place in the culture. If that is an inadequate context, the move to a desert island and build your own culture. Don't destroy mine in the process.

Chapter 7

Individualization

From the beginning of time, the nuclear family has been the basic social unit. It was true in the Garden of Eden and it is true today. While the family has transcended time and space, its context has changed over time.

In the Hunter-Gatherer culture, the family was dependent on the interaction of the tribe. Hunting required the cooperation of all of the men in the tribe, while the gathering and preparation of food and clothing required the cooperation of the women. All that changed in the advent of the Agricultural Age, when the family farm was the context of the family. The size of the family was relative to the economics of the setting. A large family was good, for it increased the hands to do the work and made the family wealthier with the increased size of the family. In that setting, no one had the option of independence. Everyone had to contribute to the welfare of the whole. And no one could be dependent. Everyone had to pull their own weight and fill their role. All were a necessary part of a greater whole.

The relational model was not independence nor dependence, but interdependence. The unit (family) functioned as one organism, each part existing as the part of a common life. To some degree, there was a merging of identities into the greater whole: The family.

The industrial age began the process of reshaping the family. Dad no longer worked in the field with the boys, but went off to the factory by himself as the rest of the family learned to live at least 8 hours a day without him. The roles shifted to accommodate this change of context and humanity was moving surely toward a change in the individuals in the family and the family itself. Before long, war broke out and Dad was off to war and mom was summoned to the factory to produce the mechanism of war. Childhood changed dramatically in just a few years in our nation as the school became the primary stable social setting in many families. The influence of the male and female role models was being replaced by the peer group and by new social constructs. Children were no longer spending all their time with their parents but were venturing into the modern school system and its increased role in their lives, and the peer group was increasingly important in the development of ideas, attitudes and influence.

Today, everything has changed from the family of the agricultural setting. In some sub-cultures in our world, there is no male father role model. The nuclear family is dead. Mom has the children alone, raises them as best she can while they are schooled, not by parents or even by teachers, but by street gangs and TV violence. The interdependence of the family members of the past has been replaced by an individualism, both in context and in the roles in our media.

Even in our normal greater culture, the family has changed. The children no longer play games with their siblings or neighbors in the back yard or in the streets. Their activities are organized into classes, leagues, and structured social systems outside of the family. Little League, Pop Warner, Karate, sports leagues, performance venues, dance classes, music classes, and a host of other items of personal development and individualized interests leave mom driving a thousand miles a week delivering and picking up the children, who no longer have mutual interests or family time. They are attending individualized classes in school and developing individualized interests outside of school. In their spare time, which is little, that are texting their peer group, talking on their personal cell phones and playing individual games on their personal computers. The family may live in the same house, but it is no longer interdependent, merged into a singular unit or relating as individuals who are part of a singular whole.

The end result is the emerging of official solutions to human problems to replace the relational solutions of the past. In the past, if the neighbor's barn burned down, the entire community turned out to have a 'barn raising.' Today, we hear about it on the evening news, think it is sad and hope they had insurance. The insurance corporation hires the construction corporation who gets a government loan with a government mortgage insurance rider and everything is handled without community involvement at a relational level. We do not know our neighbors and if we did, we would probably have little common interests anyway.

The social contexts and interdependence of the past has been fractured into a million pieces and it will probably not go back anytime soon. So, we no longer take care of human problems and needs at a relational level. It is all at a structured governmental level. And that has become our greatest problem and challenge. The distant structured program has too little knowledge about the real individual problems to be effective or to have a heart in dealing with them. The more distant the relationship, the less effective is the help. The more structured the official program is, the more it costs. The less personal the program, the greater is the possibility of scams, created dependence and ineffective waste.

It is in the family that we are forced, for the sake of survival, to give and take, merge our goals into a central relational motion. It is in the sanctity of marriage that we have to submit our individuality to the good of the greater whole and to become more in the union that we would be as the individual. Synergy is the phenomenon in which the whole is greater than the sum of the parts. The family takes on an identity and energy in which the end result is worth the loss of individuality by the values gained from the relationships. It requires sharing, give and take, care and concern, not just for the 'me' but for the effect of 'us.' The family is still the best place to find the glue of social interaction, the power of united interdependence and the wonder of love. Its values are enormous.

The loss of the family has cost us a lot. Children from broken homes do not do as well in school, in work or in their adult social life. The learned independence and sense of selfishness predisposes one to see all relationships in terms of how they affect the "me." It is in the family that the 'me' gets to stand down, see the other individuals and accommodate life in its greater whole.

Family development requires that individuals lay aside their individual interests to include the interest of another. It is the merging of personalities, goals and desires into one, as is the Christian model – "These two shall become one." Watching older couples who have been married for many years will emphasize this phenomenon as they seem to think together and, in many cases, even look alike. There is something transcendent in this merging and the resulting power of the relational unit.

Family structure may have variables, but inevitably the family will take on individual roles in the merged identity and a hierarchy will develop with an alpha figure, usually male as in most all of nature, and the nurturing female role of mother. A minister friend used to use the illustration of Johnny cutting his finger and coming into the house crying. Mother says, "Oh my poor baby. Come to mommy and I will kiss it and dress it and make it better." Dad looks over the situation and realizes in is not life threatening and says, "Johnny, get a paper towel and wrap it up and stop bleeding on the carpet."

The minister asks which response is the right one. The answer is, both. Each role is needed to make a rational whole. The child needs both the emotional support and the rational direction to become fully human. And in both cases, the parent needs to be the parent. Without the structures of authority in the home, Johnny will have to learn them later from the official authority and the cost will be greater. In some settings, the only father role model is the police, and that is totally inadequate. The police should never have to do for the family what the father should have done. It is not fair to the police and it is certainly not fair to the child.

Homeostasis (or relational equilibrium) refers to the continuity of a system, a steady internal state of a system that is maintained through regulation, the use of family norms, and mutually reinforcing communications. In the family of the past, roles were determined by gender. That is yet true in most of nature, but in our modern individualized world, that is not popular. The emergence of the woman's rights movements and the breakup of the family has led to the sissyfication of the modern male and the emergence of the sufficient female who seems to need to prove that she can take on the world without the weight of a wimpy guy to tow around. Yes, we have lost the traditional family model, but we have lost much more. We have lost the equilibrium of the basic unit of social strength, the family.

Family resources have traditionally been the strength of our society. People are most likely to turn to their families for support when in crisis and in need. With the absence of the family system to support the individual in crisis, we have to appeal to some official governmental resource, which, even if available, has no heart and no soul. It is official not relational. It can stuff us into the system and give us the end result, but it cannot care and cannot see the undercurrents of emotions and causes that are exposed in the relational family setting.

The family also creates meaning. It defines the greater sense of what the world is, who we are and what we can expect in life. It provided the basic construct of identity for the individual in the discovery of skills, talents and life's roles. It engenders trust, love, and compassion and envisions the realities of God, honor, truth and responsibility. It is the best place to discover and relate to the ethics of relationships, the morality of personal dignity and the truthfulness of trust.

- From 1901 to 1970, the divorce rate increased by 700%. In 1900 there were 56,000 divorces in America; in 1992 1.2 million, a 700% increase, adjusted for population growth (Insight 6/17/96, p. 14)
- From 1970 to 1992, the divorce rate increased 279%; the number of children with a divorced parent increased 352%, the cohabitation population increased 533%, which means 2.7 million unmarried households, 40% of them containing children. (Stanton, pp. 2-3)
- Within six months of their marriage, 50% of newlyweds begin to doubt the marriage will last, 39% report "big fights" at least once a week and 4% had already separated for at least one night. (Philadelphia Inquirer, 1994)
- "Between 1970 and 1995, . . . the percentage of married couples with children dropped by a third, but single-parent families nearly doubled." (Larry Witham, "New data on American family offer few hopeful signs," WT National Edition, March 11-17, 1996, p. 1)
- In 1960, 243,000 children were living with a single parent who had never married; by 1993 this figure had risen to 6.3 million.
- 1.2 million Children per year are born into fatherless homes. America has 1.8 million

"latchkey" kids. (Seven Promises of a Promise
Keeper, p. 118)

- 20 years ago, 17% of American children grow up
  without a father; today, 36% do.
- In 1960, 8 million children were living only with
  their mother; in 1995, 23 million.
- Three fastest growing forms of the family in the
  US, 1980-95: 1. Single mother families; 2. Blended
  families (step-parents); 3. Divorced families (the
  family left over after divorce). (Stanton, p. 1)

Follow along with some more statistics: Research has now
established a clear link between the breakdown of the
family and the major problems plaguing our society.
Consider the following facts:

- Divorce is the leading cause of childhood
  depression. (National Institute of Child Health and
  Human Development)
- 75% of adolescent patients at chemical abuse
  centers are from single-parent families. (Center
  for Disease Control, Atlanta, GA)
- 63% of youth suicides are single-parent children.
  (Center for Disease Control, Atlanta, GA)
- 70% of teen-age pregnancies are single-parent
  children. ("Children in Need: Investment
  Strategies for the Educationally Disadvantaged" -
  Committee for Economic Development.
- 75% of juveniles in youth correction facilities are
  from single-parent families. (Bureau of Justice
  Statistics, 1988)
- Children of divorce are 5 times more likely to be
  suspended from school; 3 times as likely to need

psychological counseling; 2 times as likely to repeat a grade; are absent from school more, late to school more often; show more health problems. (Dr. Gene Brody - Study of Competence in Children and Families; Gormely, Newburgh, NY) The question is, are people happier now that we live in an age in which divorce is easy, quick and socially acceptable? Does the fact that divorce was not an option to our parents and grandparents, mean that they were unhappy in their marriage and that we are better off in our individualized world? Is the end result of the carnage to our children and their world an acceptable cost for our not learning to submit our individuality into the context of the greater whole of the family?

As goes the family, so goes the community. As goes the community, so goes the nation. We are experiencing serious challenges to our national structures, our economics and our continued existence as a culture. At the foundation of all of these issues is the loss of our family structure and the individualization of our world. If we cannot regain the sanctity of marriage and the family values of our traditions, we are doomed. If we cannot assimilate the structures of the relational setting of the home, then we will not be able to cope with the official structures of government. When individualization moves to its illegitimate extreme, it will find the crisis of a clash with the law and both will lose. If we cannot build the home and the family then we will have to build more jails, more programs and confiscate more taxes. There is tremendous cost to the nation for our loss of the family.

The family is the mirror through which our identity is formed and that reflection, if absent will result in the confusion of role, goal, even gender identity. The value of this sacred and historic unit cannot be over emphasized. It is the basic currency of life.

Chapter 8

Assimilating the Purpose

Much energy is wasted in trying to find a purpose in life.
To some degree, the purpose for all of us is born out of
the same cloth. Our purpose is the redemption of
creation. The task is translating that into an individual
identity.

Whether you believe the creation story to be literal, a
narrative, representative, allegorical, or other, the
reflection upon our human responsibility is the same.
Let's look at the picture for a moment...

Somewhere in the distant past, creation suffered from the
rebellion of Lucifer and those angels who followed him.
He, who was the second in command to God Himself,
decided that he was equal to God and stepped forward to
take his place. Arrogance is a very dangerous thing! His
penalty was to be cast to the earth, the loss of access to
the heavens and the stripping away of his position.

Several of the Biblical prophets provide us with the
picture of this being cast to earth and of the tragedy that
followed. Genesis paints the picture of the earth
becoming without form and void. Others tell us that the
penalty was not just isolation from the universe, but that
Lucifer was cursed to become but dust on the earth. He
was given the sentence of losing his ascendant position
even on the earth and to be ground to dust on the earth.

In this picturesque story, God steps to the earth also, and
in the presence of Lucifer, takes a hand full of the dust of

the earth and breathed into it His breath of life. The resulting creature, this dust person was then placed in the garden of God and given rulership of the garden and of the earth. God did, of course know, that Lucifer was present and in the garden. He did know that human kind was about to undergo the temptation and the fall. Man would, in ignorance and passion, give over his rightful place to Lucifer.

Yet, that is not the end of the narrative. It is only the beginning of the end for Lucifer. The statement being made in the creation of man is that God can take from the dust of the earth, which Lucifer will become, and replace him as seated with God in heavenly places. In fact, the dust man that God created is the destined instrument of the final epitaph of Satan. He, Lucifer, will bruise his heal, but mankind will crush his head. The purpose of God in the creation of man is to make us the instrument of His hand in grinding Lucifer to dust and replacing Him as the commanding representative of God in creation.

Now that is a grand and high calling. That is a purpose worth envisioning. We are warriors, soldiers, if you will, marching onward through history, learning how to administer the principles of heaven into the human systems on earth and into the lives we touch. It is grand. It is glorious. It is also difficult. God did not just wave a magic wand and make everything perfect. That is our job.

And it is here that we have to stretch our mind a bit. The problem we face is a fallen perspective of reality and an assumption that we can wait until God makes everything perfect. But that was the purpose of Christ on the cross.

He made all things new. He provided access for us into
the throne room of the eternal, but He did not take away
our will or the need for us to grow into the position we
have been given. That is a process, not an event. It is that
process that we seem to keep messing up. We seem to,
like Israel of old, moving toward the Promised Land, turn
an 8-day journey into 40 years. We keep wandering and
going around the mountain and reverting to the elements
of the curse and missing our role in the redemptive
process.

For a more complete treatment of this subject, I
recommend, The 'King of the Earth,' by Eric Sauer,
Dynamix Worx press.

Chapter 9

Assimilating the Context

> I Samuel 8:4 Then all the elders of Israel gathered together and came to Samuel at Ramah, 5 and said to him, "Look, you are old, and your sons do not walk in your ways. Now make us a king to judge us like all the nations."
>
> 6 But the thing displeased Samuel when they said, "Give us a king to judge us." So, Samuel prayed to the Lord. 7 And the Lord said to Samuel, "Heed the voice of the people in all that they say to you; for they have not rejected you, but they have rejected Me, that I should not reign over them. 8 According to all the works which they have done since the day that I brought them up out of Egypt, even to this day—with which they have forsaken Me and served other gods—so they are doing to you also. 9 Now therefore, heed their voice. However, you shall solemnly forewarn them, and show them the behavior of the king who will reign over them."

Ancient Israel models in this passage the history of humankind in our search for justice, authority and social sanity. God provided relational structures to context our human identity, but that was not enough for us. We had to formalize our social structures and organize them so as to guarantee justice, goodness and government. The problem is, that the more we move away from relational solutions to human problems, the more we invite a depersonalization of authority and the hierarchy of human power in contrast to a direct relationship with the Creator.

God instituted several points at which He would relate to mankind:

1. The Individual

2. The family

3. The church

4. The world in general

Mankind has inserted human government as a 5th arena and God has allowed it, not because it is better but because we insisted. We would be better off without that institutionalization in our experience. The plan of God was for Him to govern man directly through the counsel of the prophets and the care of the priests. But He had placed the earth under our care and thus it was our call how we decided to govern it.

With this interjection, the rule of human government, we had set up a barrier between man and God and the penetration of that formalized system of relationships tends to disallow any relationship except with itself. That is, the wayward child is better served by the discipline of the parent than the official pronouncements of a government agency. Parents provide relational correction in a context of love, acceptance and forgiveness. The governmental agency has no love, it only has laws and penalties. The only function of government is to regulate. It has no product, no money, no grace and no humor. It is, in a very real sense, without grace or soul. It is hard, callous and cold.

The illusion of mankind is that we need leadership – some strong voice of authority to find and fix problems, to create social structures that solve human problems and to move us from our restless wandering into a Utopia of perfect social relationships. But government with its laws and regulations does not create relationships, it removes the human element from the equation of human interaction and strips the interactions of it personal, face to face value. It is a substitute for our seeking the face of God and finding His wisdom in the interaction of the structures He gave us – The family, the church and the intimacy of personal relationships.

Certainly, the world is not an easy place, and there are those toward whom a defense is necessary. It is there that the formation of armies and police forces to protect us from those lawless elements has value. Yes, it is also the tendency for that collaboration of protection to grow to the point that it is, in and of itself, the intruder into our personal wealth and welfare.

For a further treatment of this subject, I recommend the short book, 'The Law,' by Frederick Bastiat. It is old, but it is a masterpiece.

The best and greatest justice is that which is obtained at the lowest level and by the highest form of relationships. The people involved in the issue that needs resolution are the ones best suited to find the best solution. When formal governmental agencies take the place of the family, the community and the individual, freedom is not well served. It never has been and never will be. Freedom is the essential element that exposes our insecurity and fear and drives us to seek the strength and wisdom of the Creator God. It is good that it should be so.

The context that God established is straightforward and simple. It is natural and profound. It is effective yet without formal documents and codified laws it is the family, living by a common life. And that is the essential difference between relational authority and formal authority: Relational authority is an organism, living by a common life, while governmental agencies are simply the organization of legal codes without life at all.

Is government then evil? No, it is not good or evil, yet tends to work within the matrix of the Tree of the Knowledge of Good and Evil. It is not evil yet is does provide a structure where those who are motivated by the will to power, can exercise their authoritarian sense of superiority. It is not good, and yet it provides a context to hold civilizations together as we wrestle with the challenge of redeeming the earth in righteousness. It is both the place to hide from our insignificance and insecurities and a place where formal justice keeps the peace within the context of those who need to fix things for us. It is the best we can do and the worst we have ever done. It is the tragedy of human searching and the comedy of human stupidity. It is only what we make it to be, but it is less, far less than what God provided.

The story of the Garden of Eden is also the continuing story of human history. Cain went out from the garden and killed his brother Abel. Rather than face the consequences of coming face to face with God, he went out and built a city. The city has always been man's covering of himself and hiding from God rather than accepting that which God has provided. It is in the restless agitated guilt and pain of existence that humanity seeks relief from the fall rather than submitting to the Creator who has it covered.

The redemption of humanity from the fall is not found in human government. It is found in the acknowledgment by mankind of our need for the continuing government of God, born out of fellowship with Him. Man, by himself, will always model his existence in the structures of earthly government and in that context will be self-sufficiently lost to the purposes of God. Our hope is built on nothing less, than Jesus sacrifice and the impartation of divine righteousness and wisdom. God has a divine compensation for every human weakness. The problem is in getting our permission to apply it.

Our search for self aside from the Creator is the ultimate absurdity. It assumes that in leaving the context of relationship with our Creator we can find that which He made. It is not God who left the context of creation but man. God is not lost – we are. We are aimless wanderers in the sea of frustration, looking for that which is found only at the feet of the Redeemer. How simple, yet how profound. How obvious, but seemingly difficult.

Chapter 10

Rebellion: Our Common Path to Frustration

In was in 1960 that Linda and I united our lives in marriage. We left the church and headed off on an adventure, on our honeymoon and into life together. We spent a week or more at Lake Tahoe and then drove across the mountains to make a brief stop at some friend's house in Oakland, CA. They smothered us with congratulations, took us to dinner and then had something important they wanted to show us. We drove across the Bay Bridge to San Francisco and to the intersection of Haight and Ashbury where scores of young people were dressed up like, well, like each other. It was blatantly weird and noticeably different from the usual dress the rest of America wore. They were called Hippies.

This was not a costume party, although it was costumed as opposed to being something of spontaneous difference. It was a statement of rebellion. They were anti-establishment, as though the rest of the world was able to be categorized as a singular synonymous whole. But

for them, the difference that normally existed in the human family were insignificant, their difference was in contrast to all the others.

They were rebelling against, well, I was not sure what. It took time for the movement to develop its agenda and to tell us, in a clear and understandable statement what they were against. They were against most of the traditions and moral and ethical restrictions of their parents and were set to break free of them. They were proposing free love, which of course Linda and I thought we had when we got married a few days before. They were proposing drugs, sex and rock and roll, which of course existed before they decided to use it as symbols of their rebellion. It was hard to understand the specifics of this somewhat illogical and incoherent set of statements, but there they were, in all of their glory, making their statement by being different and, frankly, quite weird.

Well, everyone who has a sense of the history of that movement can look back and knows in some general sense what it was about. It was about breaking away from the established moral and ethical standards of their parents, or being an in-your-face contrast to the traditional life style and forms of our social constructs. They were against the family, against marriage, against money, against property, against capitalism, against anything and everything.

Well, that was then and this is now. The Hippy Revolution came and went and, as was predictable, it worked well as long as the parents against whom they rebelled, provided the money for their rebellion. But alas, as expected, the money ran out and selling tie dyed shirts and drugs to others in the movement ran into an economic dead end. There was no sustainable economic foundation to support the philosophies of anti-philosophical freedom. Life demands some level of responsibility and not working also means not eating.

In time the movement disintegrated into the memories of those who seemingly had a good time, but who at some point in time had to face reality and go to work. The grim realities of economics ruined a perfectly good rebellion. And that is the problem with rebellion. Eventually you run out of things to rebel against.

Breaking free from one's parents is always a difficult time. All of us have gone through the same experiences of growing up and thinking our parents are some kind of gods, caring for us and providing for our every demand. We open our eyes one day and a new thought pops into our head. Ah ha! Our parents are just people, yes, and just fallible people. In fact, they are not all that cool. They have old ideas, old traditions that make little sense and they demand too much of us without any reasonable sense of modern reality. We are growing up and we are also growing out. We are becoming independent in our thinking and we begin to make contrasts between what we learn at school, from our peer group and from our parents. Soon, by the time we are about 15 years old we somehow magically become omniscient. We finally see it. Our parents are ignorant bumpkins from an ancient time where ignorance was the order of the day and they cannot understand us, now that we have accumulated the sum total of all knowledge.

Rebellion! Such a wonderful time when we challenge all truth, reject all reason and enter a world of self-satisfying narcissism. Our parents of course, had grown accustomed to our worship as little children and are not prepared for our new found wisdom, intelligence, and our need for freedom from them and their rules and expectations. So, the battle is on. We are not going to take it anymore and we do not have to submit to the values of the old and ignorant.

But hang on. This is not the final state of our growth. We are only going through another stage that we consider the pinnacle of maturity. We seem to think that we have finally arrived, but we are only entering the most dangerous time of our lives. We are entering a time when we know it all, but will find out in a few short years, that our presumptuousness was only an illusion and that we knew very little indeed about life, reality and of the fabric of living. We are at our most arrogant, but also our most vulnerable point in life. It is at this time that our parents think seriously of locking us in our closet until we are about 25 – 30 years old.

All of this is to some degree the natural result of our development and of coming to grips with our individuality. The danger is that we mistake the need for individuality and personal identity in contrast to the principles and structures of the family we are growing up in. We see the values of the parents as the enemy rather than understanding the history and experience that went into the development of those principles. We seem, in our teen age years, hell bent on learning by experience what we will not learn by instruction. We seem to have to re-invent the wheel at every turn.

The reason our parents are so frantic and unreasonable at this time is that, yes, they went through it when they were our age and they can see the pitfalls and traps. They know what they are, because they fell into them.

So, is it wise for the parents to just back off from the rebellious teen and let them fail and learn by their injuries? No, not at all. The general rule of parenting is that you have to win the contest, set the definition of sanity for the household and enforce the principles that you know to be true. If you don't win, then everybody loses. You lose your parental position; the child loses their sanity and safety and the world is filled with the fall out. Yes, this is worse than global warming, carbon footprints and the national debt. It is life and death – literally.

I was very fortunate in growing up. My parents were wiser than most and provided room for the breaking away process without allowing the principles of morality and sound ethics to be sacrificed. They seemed to be able to come along side rather than to stand only in the place of confrontation – face to face. They understood that there was an alternative position to be in and they guided from along-side. They made place for the transition from dependence to independence, by focusing on interdependence. They let me walk down the road of individuality while keeping control of the context rather than the content. They made me responsible for my actions, attitudes and future. They were exceptionally wise parents.

It is needless to say that there are some exceptions where a parent's example or demands are dangerous to follow, where pure evil exists or where the issue is not principles but confusion. What we are talking about is rebellion in the heart of the child, and we have all had our share. To reject sound principles that have been tried in the fires of history and proven true, is to invite disaster into one's life. This is not wise. To reject the traditions of generations simply for the sake of individuality does not create individuality, but only a weirdness that is unsustainable without paying a price too high to be worthwhile. You may not like the genetics that you have been given, but genetics is not a negotiable commodity. Genetics are what they are. Our behavior and how we deal with them is the issue.

Grace is the ability to take what has been given to us and to use it to make us better, stronger and more productive. Life is not about rejecting what I am and what I have been given in life, but about what I produce with it and how I shape it into something beautiful, useful and worthwhile. The self that I am is not something to run from but to embrace and shape and create. To start with, in our teen years, that shaping is best seen through the eyes of those who love us and care for us. It is most distorted by our youthful arrogance, our need to break free and yes, our hormones.

The concept of submission is not well liked in our culture. We are a nation born in rebellion and proud of our freedom and independence. But submission to good authority is our salvation while rejection of bad authority is also. The difference is not in the eye of the beholder, so to speak, but in the content of the authority. Good authority exercises only the amount of power necessary to fulfill its responsibility. Bad authority takes more power than is needed and oversteps responsibility. Too little power to fulfill one's responsibility is weakness. Too much is abuse.

The rejection of the King by the American Colonies, was founded in the understanding of our God given rights and the abuse of them by the King. That rejection, although commonly called rebellion, was not rebellion at all in that it was the rejection of tyranny and a refusal to submit to bad authority. It is not the same at all as the common youthful rebellion where parental authority is trying its best to provide protection and guidance to the child who is struggling to find a path to independence, but is stumbling over itself, not the loving care of legitimate responsibility and good authority.

Chapter 11

Telling Yourself the Truth

Many years ago, I got a notice of a special retirement meeting for our former pastor. We had been raised in the church and he had a great influence in my life, so I decided to attend, even though it was quite a distance from our house. Just a few days later I got another invitation to a reunion of retired police officers in the city where I had served. Both were in the same city and both on the same weekend. This would be tricky, but I replied to each that I would be there, and then worked on the schedule of how to work it all in as best I could. Fortunately, the events were on different days and there was no overlap, so I got to get it all in.

One of the profound things that happened was just in the social time with old friends. The church gathering was wonderful, and all the kids I was raised with were there. We laughed, talked and told and listened to a lot of old stories. Somewhere along the way, I noticed that memories were different for different people. I had assumed that an event, lived in reality would be recorded on the mind of each who were involved, with the exact same mental images. But they were not. I was included in many of the stories as the ring leader in various adventures, some of which I was not involved with at all.

To some degree, I dismissed it as their seeing me in a certain role, and whether or not I was there, their memory scanned the mental images and for whatever reason, interjected me into the role I usually had with the group. But it was more than just that, for the stories were memorable, in that I remembered the incidents, but there seemed to be a lot of elaboration, distortion and sometimes simply exaggeration. The stories were not exactly how I remembered them. But then, if their memories can be interpretive, mine might be also, I conjectured.

The next day, and for three days I was around my old COP buddies, and again, we were telling and listening to stories and laughing and remembering. But there was something essentially different from the night before. These stories were exactly as I remembered them. The interpretative and embellishment factors were not there. I thought about it for a minute and then decided that the difference was in the context. The old friends from my childhood, the night before, would be expected to tell stories with interpretations and embellishments, but these cops were trained to tell the truth, the whole truth and nothing but the truth. They were all seasoned veterans who had been in court many times and had faced the most skilled interrogators in the area – prosecuting and defense attorneys. They knew that you never wanted to get caught lying or slanting the story in court. It never had a good outcome. So regardless of what happened or how embarrassing, you told the truth – period.

While evaluating these two different settings and the experience of the stories, I thought of how it is that most people are not cops and they do not live with the same matrix of pressure to be specific and detailed in their memories. Most allow their minds to make of the events of life, whatever it needs to, to support their sense of self-value and self-worth. Few people are able to face a bad situation and to say to themselves, "You are responsible for this one buddy and only you can get yourself out of it."

The human race is bent to excuse failure and embellish accomplishments. We live in a world that is filled with victims – people, who through no fault of their own, are in conditions that they should not be in. They are not responsible and their parents, friends and counselors assure them that they are victims of what other people have done to them. The poor are in their condition because the rich have made all the money. The sick is ill because the farmer or producer, or grocer sold them poisoned food. You get the picture.

The memory is interpretive. It is usually inaccurate and over time tends to replay things in an ever-increasing circle of fuzzy embellishments. The problem is, that we believe they are true. The second part of the problem is that, once attached to our soul, those interpretations tend to paint us into victimization and excuse us from responsibility.

The message of creation is that you have been given a life to live and a potential to reach and no one will do it for you. If you do not move forward on the path to life, no one else will do it for you. One of the greatest things that can happen to any of us is to wake up to the fact that life, with all of its difficulties and pitfalls, is only going to be what we make of it. No one else will take responsibility for us and if they try to, they will, certainly and predictably, ask us to sell our soul for the care they offer.

Most people who live off of government subsistence cannot justify doing so without a process of victimization and the erosion of their sense of responsibility. When the help offered shifts from being what it is, to an entitlement (what you deserve) then you are dependent and hooked. In our modern culture we live in a world filled with entitlements, all of which require an excuse of victimization. Once the mind tells you that you are stuck in life and cannot get yourself out of the hole, you are dead to progress and success.

Being the victim is not good for any of us. Even when we are truly disadvantaged by a twist of fate or are victimized by the bully, real or by circumstances, we cannot recover if we decide to stay there and not move on. Life can never be painted in beauty when we are not in touch with the reality of our personal responsibility and our power to change the circumstances.

We all talk to ourselves. Oh, we don't go down the street, speaking out loud and then speaking answers to ourselves, but we do think, process and explain the world we experience to ourselves. We make decisions, long before we act on them and long before they are spoken. We arrange facts, calculate data, evaluate processes, accumulate information and store it all in the central processing unit – the brain.

The brain is the storage unit for raw objective facts, but it is also the subjective mechanism by which we interpret our world, determine our objectives, set our course and form our opinions. Sometimes it is not so much what we think as how we think. Most often two separate individuals can live in the same environment, experience very similar experiences and yet form very different opinions. For some, the brain is not stimulated to fire the synapsis and engage the endorphins without some physical activity. For others the excitement of life comes through reading a good book or doing a challenging puzzle. We are all different in our emotions, our thoughts and the kinds of things that are important to us.

What this gives rise to is the vast differences we see in the human family. No two people have the same fingerprint, the same eye iris or the same responses. We live in the same proximity to one another yet come away with very different conclusions.

In that process, we interpret our world, not just in an objective fashion, but subjectively. We may agree that the ocean is blue, but when asked the meaning of that, we may each assign a different meaning to the conclusion. Politics is a good example. If we say the economy is in bad shape and we need to do something, what shall we do? Those with a liberal mindset may suggest that we raise taxes, create more government programs to take care of people while the economy is bad, targeting the least damage to the most vulnerable. Those from the right might suggest that we lower taxes so the private economy has more money to circulate to create more jobs so that people effected by the poor economy can work and make a living. Same problem, but two opposite approaches in responding to it.

The same is true in psychology, religion, ethics, and any discipline you can name. Given the same set of circumstances, two people may come up with very diverse responses, attitudes and actions. Part of that is probably genetically controlled and we are, well stuck with it. But part of it is our personal interpretation of the objective facet, as it is filtered through our attitudes and opinions. What we can do is learn to judge our attitudes and opinions and to adjust them by the objective reality we know and thus alter the end result of the process.

Let's look at several areas where we may miss the greater reality in this process.

1.   Defensiveness.

We are born into this world totally helpless and vulnerable to the terror of existence. We are totally dependent on our parents and know only the security that we receive through them. As we grow, we learn to relate to our world incrementally and yet, through the matrix of our parents' care. If our parents are wise, they allow us to experience life in the process of growing up, as much as we can handle but not too much too fast so that we are secure and safe.

The problem is, we are insecure, that is, if we are wise. For left to ourselves at too early an age, we would not survive the ravages of nature. We somehow have the illusions of Mother Nature as a kindly soul, carefully taking care of each one of us. But Mother Nature is severe, unpredictable, and dangerous.

Insecurity is the defense we all start with as we walk carefully into our world and move through the early years of life. But for some, insecurity is never left behind. Whether it is how we were raised or our own genetic makeup, some of us remain fearful of the world, of other people and of life in general. It is this insecurity that gives rise to needing to defend ourselves against our enemies. Yet, it can distort reality into a grotesque panorama of enemies, all of whom are after you in the night. It is this defensiveness that places barriers between us and others and between us and the enjoyment we might otherwise experience in our world. Defensiveness is wise when there is real danger, but without real danger, defensiveness is the enemy itself.

2. Rejection

Everyone wants to be accepted. Particularly in Junior High School, acceptance is the singular goal of relationships. Acceptance affirms us, validates our existence and gives us a place to stand in our world. Peer acceptance becomes, in our early teens, the driving force of life. Where later in life we are able to live within our acceptance of ourselves, it takes time and experience before our existence within the world is validated by other than peer acceptance.

Rejection is difficult even in our adult experience. When a trusted friend, relative or mate rejects us and leaves a relationship with us, it is devastating. In retrospect we usually look back and see that it was not the end of the world and may even have been a good thing in releasing us to other relationships and to the world in general, but it is never easy. The reflection of rejection is the fear that the person rejecting us may be right. We may not be worthy of their relationship. The spotlight of emotions always refocuses from them to us as we allow rejection to make us feel worthless, ugly and stupid. It is usually an illusion, not reality, yet it certainly seems real in the middle of the process.

3. Fear

The base emotion of all negativity is fear. It is the basis for anger, hostility and all human emotions that move us to hide and run and excuse ourselves and move away from the path of success. Fear is the chief tool of Satan, in projecting disaster into our minds. In a spiritual and psychological sense, fear is the great enemy.

Franklin D. Roosevelt, in his great speech that launched us into world War Two, used the phrase, "We have nothing to fear, but fear itself." That is also true in our daily lives.

And we could go on enumerating a host of specific enemies that we encounter in life, but that is unnecessary. The point is, we must learn to tell ourselves the truth. It is not something that comes naturally. It is not something that the world will train us to do. It is something that will take a great deal of strength and courage. It is easier to excuse ourselves, play the victim or stand on the sideline. But that is the road to failure. When we have learned to tell our self the truth, then we are free to take responsibility and live as a king. Ruling yourself is the essence of reigning in life.

Chapter 12

You Cannot Become What You Already Are!

I was always torn by the classes I took on the influence of environment on the behavior of children and adults as well. It seemed that our behavioristic bend in psychology has given us a view of behavior as the expression of our environment, our influences and our exposure to stimulus. But since I was about 15 years old, I have been breeding and training dogs. I fell in love with my grandfather's dog, a German Shepherd named King. Later I enjoyed that love of the breed while watching RIn-Tin-Tin on TV and, well, it has been a lifelong passion. The problem is, in breeding generation after generation of dogs, my experience has predisposed me to a genetic model for animal behavior. I suspect that it is also true in humans, since we are also the product of our genetic makeup. So, on the one hand I hear the teachers espousing that the environment makes the behavior, in my experience I watch genetics play out its magic in behaviors and characteristics as certainly as cars rolling off the assembly lime from the Chevrolet plant will bear the Chevrolet emblem.

So, although I take the observations and studies of social scientists seriously, I suspect that their behavioristic model is only partially true. I also believe that the Biblical study of creation and of the plan of God shows some spiritual genetics at play. That is, what we are is determined by our genetic structure, modified by our environment and guided by the spiritual heritage that we have in relationship to our Creator. God has a role in all this, for He created it, governs it and is not absent from the purpose and plan that underscores it.

So, my view of our existence is that we are what our family, school and experiences give us as a context for our growing to adulthood. We are also at our core the expression of our genetic code that is the raw material that environment works on. Yet above it all is the perfect determined purpose for each one of us that is encoded in us by the Creator. Life is thus, not a random course of choices, but of choices that have forces behind them. Those forces are both good and evil. They are part of a grand cosmic drama being played out on this planet where we are the actors and there is more than one director, well it might be better said that there is one director and one imposter, pretending to be a director.

OK, here is my take on the issues of Satan and God and how humankind relates to these forces. These forces provide the context of life, but we determine the content. We are responsible for our life. We paint the picture.

The illusions of life are that we are destined to be, what the traps of life make us. Those traps are stops along the way that invite us to join them and to stay there indefinitely, stripping us of our true identity. Let's look at a few…

1.   You are not your behavior

Guilt is a bad feeling about yourself because of what you did. We are all familiar with it. It is that gripping sense of personal failure in that our behavior has violated our conscience. Guilt is a good thing. It is a correction in our spirit to guide us away from the behavior that created it. It says: STOP! Don't do that. What you did is not good for you or others.

Shame, on the other hand is a bad feeling about ourselves because of what we are. Shame is not good. Shame turns the behavior into an identity. It is irreversible and remains. It does not ask for a correction in behavior, but defines behavior as identity. You cannot be forgiven for what you are, but you can for what you did. Shame is the subtle twist that lies to us, telling us that we are our behavior and we are stuck with it. When bad behavior becomes shame, you are stuck.

Guilt asks for correction and forgiveness. Shame asks for nothing. It just lays there demeaning us and making us into something that we do not have to be. Guilt can be faced and forgiveness can wipe the bad behavior away, but shame cannot be forgiven because it is what we are. Shame has to be rejected. It is an enemy that we have to fight by rejecting its presence, its message and its implications.

Do not allow bad behavior to define you. Reject it and walk away from it.

2. You are not your imagination
Imagination is a wonderful tool in playing with possibilities, envisioning our future and planning our possibilities. But it can also have subtle twists. It can be a practical support for setting goals, planning our future and organizing our path. But it can also be a negative and grotesque demon of self-deprecation, self-destruction and self-hate. Controlling our imagination is essential to

good mental health. You cannot allow your wayward imagination to distort what you are or what you are becoming. We are responsible to discipline our thoughts, our mental images and the images we allow into our mind. The images of hell will destroy us if we allow them to stay in our mind.

Self-talk is something we all do. We tell ourselves who we are and what we should do and where we should go in life. If we entertain negative images, we will be drawn into them and defined by them. Similarly, if we tell ourself things that are rational, real and positive, we will be drawn into them. What you focus on, you will become like. Only you can determine what your imagination will be used for. Disciplined thinking is a determining factor in making life meaningful and productive.

3. You are not your environment

One of my best friends through my school years was in a terrible home. He had no father in the home and his mother was a certified nut case. His brother became a reflection of the environment they lived in. His two sisters gravitated to extremes in life style that were unhappy and unhealthy. He became the valedictorian of our class and a well-respected professor and writer. He did not let his environment determine his destiny.

Much of our world plays with the blame game. If there is failure, it is someone else's fault. We tend to excuse our bad behavior on some cause other than take responsibility for it. We blame the rich for making us poor, the educational system for our lack of education, the government for our lack of resources, the evil corporations for our personal failures…. We blame forces outside of ourselves, for what we are. It is an excuse for living in shame. DO not excuse your failure. Take responsibility for your life and make it work.

There are thousands of stories of those who have overcome tremendous obstacles to do the impossible in life. They are those who do not allow their fate to become their identity. I know this because I was raised by a father who was severely handicapped. Having polio at an early age left Dad with a debilitating limp. He was unable to walk far and could not run or jump or move like other people. He also missed a couple of years of school and was never chosen to be on a sports team. But do not refer to him as handicapped – not to his face. He never allowed his physical limitation to excuse his success. If anything, it was the force that drove him to try harder, drive with greater determination and to find ways of doing things that compensated for the disability he was given.

My good friend Dan Brophy of Pointman Ministries was shot through the neck in Viet Nam. It left him paralyzed from the neck down and confined to a wheel chair. He is one amazing guy. He hunts, fishes, drives, and does basically anything anyone else does, but has to find unique and different ways to do it. He is an inspiration to everyone who knows him. Don't tell Dan he is handicapped. He is simply unique in how he succeeds.

You are only your environment if you allow yourself to be.

4.   You are not your feelings
We all have a broad range of feeling and emotions in life. Sometimes we are sad and sometimes happy. Sometimes

we are engaged in life and sometimes we feel like giving up. If we allow our emotions to be our identity, we will be as unstable as the broad range of emotions available to us in life. The issue of emotions is not what they mean but who is in charge of life, me or my emotions. To be more than how I feel, I have to decide that I can have emotions without being my emotions. I do not have to act out what my emotions tell me. I can make a conscious determined decision to control my emotions rather than allow them to control me.

There is a wonderful story about an old man who is checking into a rest home and the nurse tells him she will take him to his room, and that she hopes he will like his room. He tells the nurse, "Oh, I love my room!" She corrects him and tells him, "But you haven't seen it yet." He comes back with, "That has nothing to do with it. I have already decided I love my room. I do not have to see it to make that decision." What a great attitude. It is our attitude about life that determines our emotions and provides us with the emotional framework for success. We are responsible for our emotions. We choose our attitude.

And we could go on in talking about various aspects of life, and existence, but there is one final overpowering issue that we need to understand. It is:

5. You are what God says you are

I mean, after all, He is the Master Creator and as such ought to know what He made. It does not necessarily follow that the creature knows better than the creator. What we come to understand about ourselves is a reflection of the reality we see in a mirror, though distorted. The Creator, knowing the end from the beginning, sees perfectly and is far more accurate than just flailing around in life trying to find ourselves. The focal point of all human identity should begin and end in finding the nature and purpose of the Creator.

He is not averse to your discovering what He made, although you have to be able to perceive through His eyes to get an accurate picture. That is not a problem, for God is not distant, mischievous nor is He hiding yourself from yourself. He wants you to know, to understand and to experience the joy of being fully you. But first He has to clear from our eyes the distortions that we have because of our fallen humanity. All we like sheep go astray. We accumulate far more information about reality from our surroundings and from the culture around us than we do from the Creator God. Therein is the problem. We are blinded by sin and see distortions through the lens of our worldliness.

If what we tell ourselves about ourselves is different from what God says about us, then it reveals not God's mistake, but our blindness. Let's take a brief look at what God says about us...

> Jeremiah 29:11 - For I know the plans I have for you," declares the Lord, "plans to prosper you and not to harm you, plans to give you hope and a future.
>
> - ➤ Genesis 2:16 – You are free
> - ➤ I Corinthians 1:30 – You are in Christ Jesus

- ➢ I Corinthians 3:9 – You are God's field, God's building
- ➢ I Corinthians 3:16 – You yourselves are God's temple
- ➢ I Corinthians 3:21 – All things are yours
- ➢ I Corinthians 3:23 – You are of Christ
- ➢ I Corinthians 4:10 – You are strong, you are honored
- ➢ I Corinthians 6:19 – Your bodies are the temple of the Holy Spirit
- ➢ 2 Corinthians 3:3 – You are a letter from Christ
- ➢ Galatians 4:7 – You are no longer a slave but God's child
- ➢ Galatians 4:28 – Now you are children of promise
- ➢ Ephesians 2:19 – Consequently you are… fellow citizens with God's people and also members of His household
- ➢ Ephesians 5:8 – You are light in the Lord
- ➢ Hebrews 5:6 – You are a priest forever…

Although the Bible is clear is condemning certain behavior, the tone used to describe the children of God is always positive, uplifting and filled with love. How else can the Creator feel toward His creation? He created us with His own hand, devised for us an eternal purpose, set us in a high calling and determined a future for us that is beyond our comprehension. There is no way to find condemnation in the scripture. Romans 8:1 assures us that – There is therefore now no condemnation to those who are in Christ Jesus…

Give the evidence of what God thinks about you, why would anyone run from it? The better course of action is to find our identity in Him and to walk out the great high calling that He has for us.

6.   You cannot become what you already are

Adam and Eve were given the same standing with God. He walked and talked with them in the garden, treated them as friends, provided everything they needed, yet He refrained from controlling them. He created us to be partners with Him in the ongoing work of creation. He made us capable of knowing Him and relating to Him and being His friend. He did all that out of the overwhelming essence of His being: Love.

Yet, Adam and Eve were sold a lie which appealed to their need to explore their freedom. The lie from Lucifer was that they could be as God, knowing good from evil. The rest is history. The remnants of Adam and Eve's quest remains within the human family. We somehow suppose that if we simply trusted God and obeyed His commands, we will be cheated out of life, or some grand experience that brings us greater promise. But the record of history is always the same. Our disobedience does bring us the knowledge of good and evil, but it also brings us, while we are pursuing the full pleasure of life, the full pain of life.

Why is it, I wonder, that we humans are so gullible and so wayward that we need to repeat history generation after generation, and never come to the understanding that

God's way are so much better and His purpose for us is sure and steadfast, certain and wonderful?

And so, we struggle to find reality, to find ourselves and to experience life apart from the plan already given to us by God. You see, the struggle and searching and uncertainty is not the solution to life's problems, it is the problem. The answer is in ceasing from the struggle and resting in the certainty of God's love and His perfect plan for us. **You cannot become by human struggle what you already are in Christ.**

Chapter 13

Integrity

Integrity is defined as:

> 1. Possession of firm principles: the quality of possessing and steadfastly adhering to high moral principles or professional standards

> 2. Completeness: the state of being complete or undivided

> 3. Wholeness: the state of being sound or undamaged

Integrity is that state of being in which all elements of one's person are integrated into a singular mind, emotion and will. Most people struggle with life because their emotions argue with their mind, trying to rationalize their behavior, or trying to give themselves permission to do something they know to be wrong, or in whatever way, doing war with themselves internally. When the mind has to be convinced that an action is legitimate, we are in trouble.

Integrity is that state of being in which the person is whole, complete, integrated and all parts of the personality are moving in the same direction. Peace is the result of integrity. One will never be at peace with their world or with themselves as long as the struggle inside is raging. Most of our personal problems are not caused by the circumstances of life, outside of ourselves, but with the lack of integration inside.

Colossians 1:21 - Once you were alienated from God and were enemies in your minds because of your evil behavior.

Ephesians 4:22 - You were taught, with regard to your former way of life, to put off your old self, which is being corrupted by its deceitful desires; 23 to be made new in the attitude of your minds; 24 and to put on the new self, created to be like God in true righteousness and holiness.

Philippians 2:5 - Let this mind be in you which was also in Christ Jesus, 6 who, being in the form of God, did not consider it robbery to be equal with God, 7 but made Himself of no reputation, taking the form of a bondservant, and coming in the likeness of men. 8 And being found in appearance as a man, He humbled Himself and became obedient to the point of death, even the death of the cross. 9 Therefore God also has highly exalted Him and given Him the name which is above every name, 10 that at the name of Jesus every knee should bow, of those in heaven, and of those on earth, and of those under the earth, 11 and that every tongue should confess that Jesus Christ is Lord, to the glory of God the Father

This is where our relationship with Jesus, the Savior, comes in. The presence of God in our lives is there to remove the blinders of the world and the deception of the enemy from our minds. The battle for good and evil is in the mind and in the emotions. When they are influenced by evil, they lie to us and split our mind from our emotions, our will from our mind –disintegrating to personality and trying to turn parts of our self against the rest of us. It is that internal confusion that is the seed plot for satanic rule and damage to our life. It is the integration of the personality in Christ that allows us to come to peace and to integrity. Integrity is the foundation for progress, peace, success and living a life in which the sense of self is not questioned but determined.

The end result of integration is seen by people as integrity and character. To have character is to be known as a person who is truthful, sound, sensible, trustworthy. My Dad was one of those guys who people instinctively trusted. He kept his word. He distrusted written contracts, preferring to look a person in the eye and shake their hand in agreement. For him, that was the swearing of an oath man to man that established a covenant of trust. He wanted to deal with people of character and integrity for he was a man of character and integrity.

Today this way of doing business is long gone. No one trusts others, for we have degenerated as a culture and society into a new, but not better world. We learn today, that you cannot trust people and that they are out to scam you. We do not respect people personally because we have become a people who lack integrity, character and truthfulness. It is sad that we have come to this kind of world.

But for the person who builds integrity and who is together in mind, emotions and will, who has integrated their self, the world is open and ready. The world cries out for people in business, politics, sales and all endeavors of life that can be trusted and relied upon. The world is an open door for those with integrity.

Chapter 14

Determining Life

So, what can I do with all this?

There is something of a press inside of us all. We want to know things, experience life and to march into the future. God made it to be so. What I am not proposing is a lazy, "I give up" approach to life. It is built into us to seek adventure, to explore our potential and to use our freedom to grow and discover. God made it to be so. It is in that press that we experience what He has made us to be. The difference between struggling and moving forward is in the peace of God and the confidence that He is guiding us to express what He made us to be.

So, we trust that God is involved in us as we inventory our skills, talents and abilities. Some of us are natural athletes. Some cannot even see the ball coming when it hits us in the face. Some can hear symphonies in their head, while others are tone deaf and cannot carry a tune in a bucket. Some see mathematical equations in special terms and can easily come to the answer, while others have no idea how many apples are on the table without a picture. We are all different. That is the beauty of creation. No two people have the same fingerprint, the same iris pattern, the same personality or the same potential. That all men are created equal is an American phrase to describe our standing before the law. It certainly does not mean that we are all alike.

Yet, we tend to follow the leaders, look to the strong personalities, and try to fit in and to be part of the group. The problem is, all groups have expectations of surrender of our will and personality to be a part of the definitions of the group. Whether written or just implied, they are always there. We tend to submit to the lies of Satan, and the demands of conformity to the group and make it our identity. If the strongest personality dresses a certain way, we all follow and call it style. It the leader gets a tattoo the group follows. It becomes a trend, a culture and ends up moving a whole group of people into an adoration of identity, until we wonder where is God and when did we leave Him to follow some guru, whom we thought gave us hope and a promise, but was lying to us all the time.

It is in your uniqueness that your identity is found and it is in the act of developing it that you find both yourself and God.

So, what do you want to do with your life? The answer to that question is probably the voice of God speaking through you. What skills and talents did He give you? Our skills, talents and desires are a great indicator of who you are in Him.

Plan, envision, dream and allow the shape of who you are to become apparent.

Few people fail because the reach too high or try too much. Most of us fail because we stand idly by and watch the world pass by without participating. If you try and fail, you have not damaged your image of self, you have only found what you should not do, or more likely, how to not do it. Failure is not fatal; success is not permanent. It is courage in action that drives us forward in life.

Life is really not all that complex. It is a series of decisions that we make all leading us from the time of innocence to a time of accomplishment. Do not get sidetracked by the lies and illusions that promise much, but leave you in bondage to an identity that is not from God, but from Lucifer himself.

If we trust in the Lord, then we have the mind of Christ. We can test our mind and judge our emotions by the standards of the Gospel. God will never lead us into sin or to be dishonest or to violate His word. But we can trust that he will and has, given us His mind and His plan for us. With that, we can live freely, love deeply, act in confidence and see the frustrations of life, move away from us as we face them and move past them.

Life is not easy. Success is not without effort. We have been given the task of working at allowing what we are to be revealed and appreciated in a competitive world. Personal responsibility will move us forward. Integrity will keep us from straying off course and reliance on the presence of God will be our strength and our reward.

So, go out there and live. Do not be intimidated by the complexity of our world or by the confusion it offers. Walk straight, stay clean, and let Christ be your companion and guide. What you are will be revealed and will bring you to a life of peace and beauty.

www.ingramcontent.com/pod-product-compliance
Lightning Source LLC
Chambersburg PA
CBHW052202150726
48002CB00003B/1085